CARING FOR
THE WHOLE PERSON

E. Anthony Allen, MD

Caring for the Whole Person

121 East Huntington Drive, Monrovia, California 91016, USA

E. ANTHONY ALLEN, M.D., M.DIV., MRCPSYCH., IS PART-TIME
RESEARCH AND DEVELOPMENT CONSULTANT FOR THE COM-
MUNITY WHOLE-PERSON HEALTH PROGRAM OF BETHEL
BAPTIST CHURCH IN KINGSTON, JAMAICA, WEST INDIES. HE
ALSO PRACTICES PSYCHIATRY WITH A SPECIAL EMPHASIS
ON HOLISTIC HEALTH. HE IS A THEOLOGIAN WITH A STRONG
INTEREST IN SOCIAL ACTION.

Caring for the Whole Person
E. Anthony Allen
ISBN 0-912552-93-X

Published by MARC, a division of World Vision International, 121 East
Huntington Drive, Monrovia, California 91016-3400, U.S.A.

All Scripture quotations, unless otherwise indicated, are from the Revised
Standard Version of the Bible, copyright 1946, 1952, 1971 by the Division
of Christian Education of the National Council of the Churches of Christ in
the USA. Used by permission.

Contents

1

The Dilemma

On Being a Healer and a Christian at the Same Time

"How do you manage to be both a Christian and a psychiatrist?" I have often been asked that question. The labels sound self-contradictory—almost an oxymoron, like Christian agnostic or honest deceiver.

As Christian health professionals, we have all struggled with a use of language that demonstrates this critical dilemma, pitting God against science. The dilemma is one of identity. In other words, exactly what is a "Christian health professional?" Is he or she a split personality—a person who by coincidence happens to be both a Christian and a health professional?

It depends upon how we define these categories. Semantics is praxis—that is, our explanations reflect our acts. The meaning of our language speaks worlds about our actions. And even beyond the semantics, is the Christian health-care professional a living contradiction?

Confusion abounds in Western-influenced health-care systems, and within the Christian church—confusion about the meaning of the words "health," on the one hand, and "salvation" as a religious term, on the other.

MY OWN STRUGGLE

As a pre-teen, I was encouraged by my family and church to make a decision to accept Christ. This was because I felt urged to ask, "What exactly is the meaning of the word 'salvation'?" Fortunately, my childlike faith allowed God to sustain me through the drawn-out explanations and struggles of life until I started training to become a health professional.

My high school and early university years involved leadership in the Student Christian Movement and participation in the InterVarsity Christian Fellowship. As a medical student, I had to face the question "What is health?" Sure enough, I thought I had the answer in my hospital training, as well as the answer to "What is salvation?"

But then the confusion started. I began to feel split apart. On Sundays I would visit the hospital and witness to patients as part of my student group. Yet on Mondays, in the same wards, I would be helping to treat "bodies." I would feel obliged not to dare to think about—much less mention—anything spiritual, lest I "offend the team" or miss some really important signs or symptoms. In fact, with this conditioning, it hardly occurred to me to think in spiritual terms at all when I was in my role as a health-care trainee.

In the midst of all this, I had a strong urge to care spiritually for people and to see their lives really turned around. So I began thinking about becoming a pastor.

PATCHWORK REPAIR JOBS

Medicine, as I was learning it, seemed too much like a series of patchwork repair jobs. The confusion became worse during my internship. Once, while I was trying to save the life of a young woman in the final stages of renal failure, a student nurse put the screens around the dying patient and prayed her into eternity. Was that audacity or being a Christian health professional?

During my psychiatric residency, while struggling with the task of being a health professional, I felt a zeal to help people really change their lives—which is how I understood the goal of the gospel. That zeal was being blighted, however, while I was doing back-breaking work under inadequate conditions. I was becoming frustrated because I was only helping the very ill to "cope," and the less ill to return merely to their former level of coping or to achieve for them whatever limited growth seemed possible.

The idea of what salvation meant in practical terms became more and more elusive. At the same time, "health" seemed more and more like patchwork.

MEDIC OR PASTOR?

Eventually, I decided to enter the Christian ministry. This was partly in order to discover exactly the nature of this "salvation" that I had experienced through my child-like faith but had difficulty sharing as a Christian health professional.

Fortunately, God had other plans for me than to leave medicine completely. He helped me to resolve some of my confusion and thus to become a more aware and a more fulfilled Christian health professional.

I share this personal illustration with you to demonstrate the problem that many of my Christian colleagues must also experience. I took the drastic step of career change that I did, not only to clarify my theology, but principally because I felt a call of God to the working out of a particular ministry. This has resulted in the part-time work I am now doing in churches as a community whole-person health consultant and the work of helping denominations in Jamaica to develop church-based healing ministries.

Yet earning a theology degree, and "doing theology" in the process, was also the means of beginning to unravel the confusion in language—and therefore in practice—which beset me. For me, at least, this confusion had made health care seem like unconnected pieces and the religious concept of "salvation" irrelevant. I had to seek to understand the meaning of salvation.

I realize, of course, that most of you may not have gone through the same kind of experience I have had, because now, some twenty years later, we have new terms like "biopsychosocial," terms like "wellness," "wholeness," and "transformation." Hopefully, this will make it easier for the Christian health professional today to avoid a split in his or her personality or in his or her thinking and acting.

And it should also make it possible for us to garner more support from one another, as well as from the church, in our ministry.

2

The Whole Person

What Science Can Tell Us
About the Nature of Being Human

In this and the following chapters we want to lay a foundation for holistic ministry. This we will do by comparing the secular and Christian perspectives.

In secular science, the starting point of whole-person health most closely approximates the beginning point of Christian experience that we call salvation. We need to examine carefully each of these points of view, beginning with the secular.

IN-DEPTH DEFINITIONS

As a starter, we recognize that health and wholeness are correlated. To appreciate them appropriately, however, we need to go farther. It is incumbent upon us to understand not only the points of departure, but also the interrelationships and implications of each aspect of these concepts.

1. *The physical aspect* of health deals with the person as matter, or as a biological object. Health and disease are defined simply in terms of preserving or disrupting the adaptive structural, physiological, biochemical or defensive systems of the body. Here, it is the laws of natural science that apply.

2. *The mental, or psychological, dimension* deals with the individual as a thinking and feeling subject. One can understand this subject only by entering into an interpersonal relationship with him or her. This is because the person is an interactive social being. Because this is true, for example, any problems in his or her socialization or nurture during childhood can ultimately lead to personality disorders and to excessive anxiety or depression, as well as contribute to the more complex addictive and sexual disorders.

One's reaction to social reality can become unhealthy because of any one or a combination of many factors. Faulty conditioning, as also an internalization of the negative feelings and disparaging evaluations of one's parents, are among the common causes of mental illness. Such defects in relationships can lead to negative concepts of self and of others. This results in inner insecurity, emotional distress and social alienation.

Psychological disorders also relate to the stressors of life. These stressors, for example, can result from demands made by the developmental stages of life, such as the mid-life crisis. Alternatively, they can take the form of unexpected trauma, such as the loss of a job, or of a loved one.

To these secular definitions, Christian health-care professionals—along with many other scientists—would insist on adding another:

3. *The spiritual or religious perspective* goes beyond the physical and the mental, or psychological. It sees the person also as spirit, receiving his or her integrity in a relationship with a supernatural being who is the creative and sustaining Agent of life and personality.

The spiritual relates to realities such as meaning and purpose, ultimate choices, individual and social morality, taboos, communion with the divine and divine providence and protection.

The spiritual person receives extraordinary enablement to transcend the limitations of the natural, of the personality, of evil and of death. Within the contexts of these elements the Deity preserves the social order and gives humanity stewardship over community as well as over the ordering and distribution of natural resources.

UNBREAKABLE LINKS

Each of these categories is interactive with the others. What challenges the health worker to break out of Western-influenced modes of thinking is the fact that the mental and spiritual are inextricably bound up with the physical, as mutually interactive parts of the whole person.

We have seen many examples of this.

For instance, the psychological factors of self-esteem, personality, social interaction style and life stressors all have an impact upon the physical. They produce symptoms in the following categories:

- somatopsychic disorders,
- autonomic disorders and fatigue related to anxiety,
- vulnerability to physical illnesses induced by life stresses,
- negative lifestyles and health habits, and
- lack of compliance with prescribed treatments.

These interactions relate to most diseases that are seen by the practitioner of physical medicine. Beyond these, however, are many psychological reactions that can produce unconsciously simulated disabilities in the form of conversion reactions (somatoform disorders). Simply put, the way we think, feel, relate and manage our lifestyle can maim us and even kill us!

The reverse, or physical to mental, image of this picture is also true. It is very possible to experience psychological reactions to physical disorders. The physical problem can affect a person's ability to define reality.

Mental retardation, for example, can result from congenital or acquired brain damage. Delirium, dementia and related psychoses (with delusions and hallucinations) can often be attributed to physiological and structural brain changes. In the same way, genetically induced psychoses can be partly related to disturbances at the biochemical level. These include the so-called functional psychoses, such as schizophrenia, and the manic-depressive psychoses (bipolar affective disorders). Physical ailments can also produce a negative reaction to being ill, or to the patient role, or to traumatic treatment procedures and merely being in a hospital.

THE SPIRIT AFFECTS, IS AFFECTED

As Dr. Paul Tournier has so well illustrated in his writings, the spiritual dimension of a person also affects his or her psychological and physical natures. (Please see the last section of this book, "For Further Reading," for recommended resources written by Dr. Tournier and others.)

At the physical level, spiritual alienation or despair can precipitate or worsen disease, or even remove the will to live. There is no doubt that spiritual crises—whether they are due to despair in God or to fear of the medicine man's hex—can kill! Conversely, there is the direct possibility of speeding up or transcending the normal healing processes through miraculous or divine healing and renewed hope.

A person's spiritual commitment toward responsibility—such as in the preservation of a healthy environment or a healthy lifestyle—can open the door to divine enablement, which positively affects that person's physical health.

An important area of interaction between the spiritual and the psychosomatic is that of spiritual rebellion, temptation and alienation. This can bring about such conditions as guilt, existential anxiety and despair, also making one vulnerable to the stress of natural, moral and supernatural evil, and leading to broken relationships. These all tend to worsen personality disorders.

FORGIVENESS AND RENEWAL

On the other hand, divine forgiveness, reconciliation, deliverance, restoration and personality renewal all bring healing of the spirit. This influences the mind and in turn promotes the healing of psychosomatic, stress-related, lifestyle disorders and any conversion-type physical incapacity.

Spiritual ill health and healing also affect social harmony and justice, both of which, in turn, have an impact on one's psychological well-being and provide resources for preventive, curative and physical health.

A further consideration about the spiritual is that stress and suffering of a physical, psychological and socio-economic nature can make one vulnerable to spiritual maladies, such as loss of faith, hopelessness and rebellion. Psychological problems can lead to sick religion. Here, for example, a crippling perception of a vengeful or over-indulgent God, or a world full only of demonic spirits, may exist as a projection of childhood conflicts or as a form of psychotic delusions.

Space does not allow us to explore exhaustively the many interrelationships among all the dimensions of the whole person, or to extend the analysis to include the socio-economic aspects of human health and experience. What is most crucial here is to recognize that mutual relationships predispose one to the existence of vicious cycles between one or more pairs of dimensions within the person.

Thus, an individual who is insecure may subject his or her body to stress by overwork and overeating. The resulting cardiac disease may lead to further stress and insecurity. Negative emotional reactions to physical illnesses (called somatopsychic disorders) can in turn affect one's response to treatment as well as retard the very will to live. Spiritual despair and loss of faith can slow the healing process of the physical or emotional illness to which one is reacting.

Science can bring us this far along the road to understanding the integrated character of human nature and existence. But our perspective remains restricted until we can define "health" more precisely, and until we can also comprehend the meaning of salvation in Jesus Christ.

3

Well-Being

The Meaning of Health and Healing

The term "health" tends to conjure up the vision of robust physical stature, at least in the mind influenced by Western thought. It commonly implies an absence of physical signs and symptoms of illness, along with normal laboratory and X-ray test results.

Rather grudgingly, the medical establishment has given some recognition to "mental health" as a valid entity. However, in order to be included in the "medical model," mental health has had to see mind as brain, and suffering as statistically validated disease classification. We can well wonder how appropriate it is for us to continue with this tendency toward a one-dimensional, materialistic view of health.

THE INTEGRAL, WHOLE PERSON

As we have seen in the preceding chapter, medical and other researchers are increasingly showing a clear mind/

body/spirit relationship in disease and health. The biblical world view has long since maintained such a unified vision of the person. So when we look in Genesis at the account of creation, the body of the person is made from the elements of nature, "dust." The person becomes a living soul because God breathes the "breath of life" into him (Genesis 2:7).

We are made in the image of God (Genesis 1:27). We have a spiritual nature. The human being is created with a mind which empowers him to name all the animals, and with a social capacity and need for a "helper" (Genesis 2:18-22). Likewise, the person was created with stewardship responsibilities, given to maintain the environment, the plants and the animals (Genesis 1:28).

The example of Christ's well-being or "wholeness" is clearly stated by the physician St. Luke in reference to our Lord's development as a boy. He says that Jesus grew mentally in "wisdom," physically "became strong," spiritually "the favor or God was upon him" (Luke 2:40).

Another biblical description of wellness and wholeness is given in 3 John 2, where St. John wishes Ga'ius wellness, saying: "I pray that all may go well with you and that you may be in health; I know that it is well with your soul." He refers to the mental and social as he expresses joy that his life stays "clean and true" and notes that Gaius sends teachers and missionaries on their way "with a generous gift" (Living Bible, v. 7).

Health in the Bible, therefore, means not just physical stature and a concession to mental well-being. Health now ought to mean "wholeness," which is an integration or harmony between body, mind and spirit; between the individual and others; between the individual and nature; and between the individual and God.

Health in its total aspect includes the biopsychosocial perspective of G. L. Engel, but goes beyond it to describe a maximum quality of life called "wellness." Because health means wholeness, it therefore does not mean merely the absence of pathology: the paraplegic person can also be whole.

IN HEALING THERE IS RELATIONSHIP

Properly considered, the meaning of the term "health" leads us, therefore, to a new semantic, calling for the terms "wholeness" and "healing." Wholeness comes not by "treating" in the narrow sense of the word, which means "acting upon" organisms as we have learned to do as health professionals. Rather, health or wholeness comes by healing.

In healing there is relationship. Healing involves a relationship on the part of the person who is being made whole with his or her healer. It also involves inner relationships with self, together with relationships with community, with nature and with God. The person being healed is an active participant in the process, in terms of expectancy, cooperation and self-help.

The meaning of healing is illustrated in Mark 5:25-30 (KJV).

And a certain woman which had an issue of blood for twelve years, and had suffered many things of many physicians, and had spent all that she had and was nothing better but rather grew worse, when she heard of Jesus, came in the press behind, and touched his garment, for she said, "If I may touch but his clothes, I shall be whole." And straightway the fountain of her blood [hemorrhage] was dried up; and she felt in her body that she was healed of that plague. And Jesus immediately, knowing himself that the virtue [healing power] had gone out of him, turned about in the press and said, "Who touched my clothes?"

Interestingly enough, this is the longest reference to a physician in the Bible, and it is the one which refers to a woman who had suffered many things of many physicians, had spent all that she had and was still no better, but rather had grown worse. What does this imply about health professionals? Is this not often still true in our contemporary experience?

"TREATMENT" IS INADEQUATE

As Christian health professionals, when we make the mistake of substituting a materialistic-technical-"treating-the-organ" approach for real healing, then we find that we are limited.

So often, I have patients coming to see me for psychological help. They complain, "Doctor, I have a financial problem now. I have been to six or seven different doctors. They have done all the different tests and they have found nothing." That reminds me of the woman!

But we are saying that healing involves a relationship. The woman reached out and touched Jesus, establishing a relationship with the healer. Healing comes partly because in that relationship there is expectancy: "If I may touch but his clothes," she said, "I shall be whole" (KJV). Healing comes because in that relationship there is the healing power of God. As healers, indeed, we are merely stewards of that power. Even in nature, God has put the power for a wound to heal. We can only work along with that process. We are not God.

So then, what does it mean to be a Christian health professional? It means that one is to be a healer rather than a treater—one who comes to Christ together with the "patient" (i.e., the person whom we serve). The Christian health professional is one who seeks to establish a healing relationship with the needy person, and in that relationship facilitate the latter's own relationship with Christ—that ultimate relationship which leads to wholeness.

"GUERRILLA WARFARE"

Without a doubt, many physicians and other health professionals have been healers in their own right over the years. It could be said that this has been a form of "guerrilla warfare," as contrasted with traditional medical battles. Because of the prevailing patchwork approach to promotion, prevention, cure and rehabilitation in health care, however, there is still need for an open victory—this on behalf of those now suffering as well as for those who will continue to suffer unnecessarily.

This is the challenge to the Christian healer and health professional. Will we embrace the new semantics and practice, or will most of us to varying degrees continue to be split personalities?

4

Christian Healing

The Meaning of Salvation in Jesus Christ

The great divide, at the level of practice, between health care and the Christian religion comes with the semantic confusion not only surrounding the word "health," but also regarding the word "salvation."

When Western thought adopted a dualism of matter and spirit in its philosophy and world view, then in one fell swoop both "health" and "salvation" ceased to have their real meaning! This dualism has compromised the caring for the whole person by medical services. It has also undermined the stated mission of spirituality in general, and of the church in particular, to proclaim and enable the true "saving" of persons.

The philosophical and theological schizophrenia of dualism has tended to alienate the practice of health promotion and care from spirituality and the Christian faith. Even where Christian denominations have been involved in health care, there has been an inadequate integration of the spiritual in medical procedures, in their hospitals and clinics.

The Christian health professional, therefore, has become condemned to living two different lives. At work, he or she does "secular" tasks only. Away from work, he or she becomes free to witness to the kingdom of God and thus encourage the spiritual growth of others. At best, many Christian health professionals may live out their faith by seeking to give high quality and ethical service. We may witness to colleagues, have fellowship with one another, give free service to the poor, or serve as short-term or long-term missionaries. We may even go so far as to slip tracts to patients or invite them to church.

COMPARTMENTALIZING MINISTRY

Yet, despite various forms of witnessing and sharing, our service may still remain compartmentalized and fail to be truly whole-person in an integrated way. We often tend to be health professionals who happen to be Christians rather than whole-person health-care givers, integrating the spiritual into our diagnosis, our patient education, cures, prevention, promotion and rehabilitation.

In a similar way, local church congregations have also tended either to abandon their ministry of healing to "secular" medicine or to divorce divine healing from medical and psychological therapy.

Both the church and the Western medical model have seen disease in terms of the individual in isolation instead of also reflecting a disruption of community or social harmony. Thus the resources of the community and local congregation as healing agents have been neglected.

Could it be that our view of salvation has failed us?

Unfortunately, but not surprisingly, in dualistic Western Christianity the concepts of sin and salvation have come to be spiritualized and moralized. Thus salvation has been portrayed in merely a forensic or law-court scenario. Sin is seen as having to do with law, rebellion, moral disobedience, guilt and punishment. Salvation from sin, therefore, involves nothing more than repentance, forgiveness, vicarious punishment (transferred from the sinner to Christ), moral transformation and striving towards moral perfection (holiness).

PERSON DIVIDED, PERSON EXPLOITED

Once Christians are morally reformed, they are left to continue in their physical, emotional and socio-economic suffering. The role of God here is seen to be only one of comforting and giving strength until death and the resurrection. Any healing in the various dimensions is to be carried out by separate professionals and their related teams. The body is left to the doctor, the mind to the psychologist, the soul to the pastor and the socio-economic to the social scientists and politicians.

It is no wonder that as history and current public life have demonstrated, the person divided is the person exploited by the dividers.

The biblical view of salvation is quite different from that conveyed in popular language and practice—even within most churches. The salvation of the Scriptures is transformational rather than simply forensic or juridical. In the Bible, to be saved means to be totally changed. Inasmuch as we have already seen healing to be total transformation, then salvation and healing are really one and the same thing.

In an ultimate sense, our relationship with God is the foundation upon which all other harmony, both within and without, becomes possible. This is God's purpose in reconciling us to himself. God's view of salvation embraces us in all our relationships. In our focus upon the God-Man mediator, we forget too often that the purpose of the cross is not only to achieve justice and propitiation, it is also to destroy sickness and suffering.

How is this corrective view of salvation represented in the Bible? We infer from the Scriptures three streams of thought.

WHOLENESS IS NORMATIVE

First, the view of wholeness as what is desired by God is normative in the Bible. The language of the gospel miracles and of the kingdom is saturated with this concept. Forgiveness is important, of course, and repentance a necessity, but the goal of each encounter with Jesus in the New Testament seems to imply complete renewal, including the restoration of sight, voice, muscular agility, liberation from evil spirits and reintegration into society (on the part of lepers and outcasts).

In the Scriptures, the person is seen as a whole being. His or her wholeness, or health, involves harmony among body, mind and spirit, between the individual, the community and the ecosystem, as well as between the individual and God. For example, St. Paul writes to the Thessalonian Christians:

> May the God of peace himself sanctify you wholly; and may your spirit and soul and body be kept sound and blameless at the coming of our Lord Jesus Christ. He who calls you is faithful, and he will do it. Brethren, pray for us. Greet all the brethren with a holy kiss. I adjure you by the Lord that this letter be read to all the brethren. The grace of our Lord Jesus Christ be with you (1 Thessalonians 5:23-28).

The letter is addressed to all the brethren in Thessalonica and embraces their well-being in comprehensive terms.

We need constantly to remind ourselves that the human person is created in God's image (Genesis 1:27), with a responsibility to live in a relationship with God and with fellow persons.

ALIENATION LEADS TO DISINTEGRATION

The second stream of thought has to do with sin and disobedience. Alienation is humanity's biggest problem, and alienation leads to disintegration.

Alienation, or separation from God (sin), occurs through doubt or being self-willed. This separation leaves the individual and his or her relationships to others out of control and leaves the environment unprotected. As a consequence, the person is rendered vulnerable to disease (or disintegration) and death (Genesis 3:19).

In other words, we become vulnerable to a disintegration of self and of relationships which, in turn, leads to disease of the body, mind and spirit—and of families and communities.

It is a person's alienation from God that leads to the problems of condemnation and spiritual guilt. Moral temptation, sins and daily guilt disrupt the harmony of body, mind and spirit, as well as a person's harmony with others. The devil's direct activity is consistently a disintegrating force.

RECONCILIATION, TO HEALING

Another evident stream of biblical teaching shows that God's act of reconciliation leads to healing. How does God save us, or meet the most basic problems of the human being? Christ's double work on the cross combats alienation and its consequent processes of disintegration by:

1) Forgiving, redeeming and reconciling, on the one hand, and
2) Healing (re-integration), on the other.

In Isaiah 53:4 and 5, the prophet anticipates the Messiah and tells us that "with his stripes we are healed." Guilt is met by forgiveness, but also with the healing of its consequences, as in the case of the paralytic (Mark 2:5-12). The Psalmist speaks of this double work of God in forgiveness and healing with the words: "Bless the Lord, O my soul, and forget do not all his benefits, who forgives all your iniquity, who heals all your diseases" (Psalm 103:2-3).

FORGIVENESS AND HEALING AT THE CROSS

What does all this tell us?

First, that the forgiveness, redemption and reconciliation of the cross bring salvation; second, that salvation also includes healing (or integration).

Through submission to God and through prayer, diseases of the body, mind and spirit can receive God's miraculous healing or health-giving harmony. Disrupted relationships can also experience the healing touch of God. Persons can become inspired and empowered to make the natural resources of medicine, as well as of social justice, available to each other.

In their writings, Paul Tournier and Robert Lambourne, both physicians and theologians, have stressed the constant association and interchangeability of the terms "salvation" and "healing" in the Bible. Indeed, the same association occurs in practice among contemporary Christian professionals and congregations. Robert G. Anderson has pointed to historical and contemporary examples of the church's mental health ministry. Ezra Griffith, a psychiatric researcher, has also demonstrated the therapeutic effects of church rituals.

As a practical outworking of their own salvation or healing, the members of a Christian congregation are called and sent by God to be a healing community through the exercise of mission and evangelism. This calling involves ministering, burden bearing and reconciling (see James 5:14-16; Galatians 6:2; and 2 Corinthians 5:18, 19). Significant skilled, trained and gifted people—both professional and lay—have been discovered in the church this way.

This calls for stewardship. Each member is called to be a priest—to take responsibility for all persons in the body of Christ and in the community at large (1 Peter 2:9).

5

Demonstrating the Kingdom

Healing as a Showcase
for Evangelistic Proclamation

We have come to understand that health is wholeness and that it is to a degree synonymous with salvation, which is the healing of the whole person. What then, are the implications for a Christian healer's understanding of evangelism? This question is particularly important for health-care professionals.

To receive salvation is to come under the kingdom, or reign of God. Here there is no separation of sacred and secular, or church and state. Also here the sacred and church serve to heal, and not to condemn or to coerce (John 3:16, 17).

Healing demonstrates the kingdom of God, which is proclaimed in evangelism.

Jesus sent his twelve disciples to heal *as part of proclaiming the kingdom of God*. Preceding the challenge to heal is the charge to "preach the kingdom" (Luke 9:2). "And they departed and went through the villages, preaching the gospel and healing everywhere" (Luke 9:6). This mandate stands for us who are his disciples in the church today.

Again, in Luke 9:11, the healings of Christ are preceded by his proclamation of the kingdom. "When the crowds learned it, they followed him; and he welcomed them and spoke to them of the kingdom of God, and cured those who had need of healing."

HEALING GIVES THE KINGDOM RELEVANCE

Too often the concept of the kingdom of God projected by the church in today's world lacks relevance. This is because we do not show the world sufficiently how the kingdom affects a person's existence in ways that can be empirically experienced or observed. Empiricism is the basis on which health-care professionals work. Indeed, should we not encourage our peers, clients and communities to put the same faith in a God who acts and transforms us as we put in medication, surgery or preventive medical and psychological measures?

Healing is both a sign and a manifestation of the kingdom power of God working through Jesus to bring his new order into existence. In this order "he must reign until he has put all his enemies under his feet" (1 Corinthians 15:25).

Healing is a natural part of the proclamation of the kingdom. Here the medium is the message! Thus the ultimate goal of healing as a sign is to point persons to the kingdom so that they may know Christ the King, or Lord, and become his subjects. Healing, therefore, is central to evangelism and is not meant to be a "secular" exercise per se.

As a microcosm or manifestation of the kingdom, Christ's healing shows that in the kingdom we are freed from the oppressive reign of sin, Satan and suffering to be under the liberating, healing reign of God. Thus, if we are laborers seeking to extend God's kingdom, and if we are truly to be vehicles of the kingdom in deed as well as in word, then healing is a necessary part of our ministry.

Where God reigns there is healing. Christ, therefore, gives the church a challenge to manifest that healing, as we proclaim the Good News of the kingdom, or reign of God, being available for whosoever will. Also, we are to proclaim the Good News as we manifest that whole-person healing which is its sign.

WHOLE-PERSON HEALING PROMOTES UNITY

Within the church itself, there is division in approaches to salvation. The Pentecostals stress the baptism and gift of the Holy Spirit, as well as divine healing. The "mainline" churches, sometimes branded "liberal" by their conservative brethren, promote social action. And the evangelicals stress personal commitment to Christ and faithfulness to Scripture.

There tends to be mutual suspicion among the three "camps" of the church. What if all three could unite their valid concerns around the needs of the whole person? That would be truly Christlike!

The reign of God among us and the related salvation of Christ involve our ministry of healing, because *the primary concern of the kingdom is the greatest good*, that is, the *summum bonum*.

Jesus Christ, in speaking of his role as the Good Shepherd, said, "I came that they may have life, and have it abundantly" (John 10:10). This is what salvation is all about! Whole person health promotion! Wellness!

In Matthew 8:16-17, as Christ cast out spirits with his word and healed all who were sick, we are reminded of the prophets' prediction of his ministry: "He took our infirmities and bore our diseases."

From the words of Christ himself we have his affirmation of the fact that his salvation is grounded in empiricism. That is, it is as real a part of the experience of the whole individual as any other reality that can be perceived by the five senses. It is here that for the Christian health professional any dichotomy between science and salvation—in terms of one being empirical and the other merely a matter of faith and attitude—breaks down completely.

In Luke 7:20-23 we see that John, like any other prophet, has his moment of doubt while in prison. He asks if Christ is really the one who is to be the saving Messiah. This is similar to the research question of any scientist. Does a phenomenon exist or not? Christ faces the research question not merely with speculation, an appeal to blind faith, or referral to the infallibility of Scripture or religious doctrine. For him, salvation is not merely a doctrinal issue but an empirical one. He presents the evidence. The writer of the gospel notes that they are asking the question at the very time when Jesus "cured many of diseases and plagues and evil spirits" (v. 21).

Next, Jesus further advances the case for empiricism. He seeks the publication of the evidence. He invites the witnesses to tell John not only what they have heard but also what they have seen. Jesus says, "The blind receive their sight, the lame walk, lepers are cleansed, the deaf hear, the dead are raised up, the poor have Good News preached to them" (v. 22). As with any empiricist, the publication of evidence is for the purpose of seeking verification of the existence of the phenomenon being questioned. Thus Christ now says, "Blessed is he who takes no offense at me" (v. 23).

Has attending to the needs of persons with health problems been a part of our proclamation and working out of the kingdom of God in today's world? Or is our work a one-dimensional, secular exercise? How much have we as Christian health-care professionals been guilty of diminishing others' awareness of the scope of the kingdom—and thus of their possibilities of wholeness—by separating our evangelism from our efforts at health-care delivery? How much have we invited patients and communities to "taste and see that the LORD is good" (Psalm 34:8)?

If we are to take Scripture as a basis of our functioning, then it becomes apparent from the verses in Luke that one theological cornerstone of our commitment to the church's ministry of integrating the proclamation of an empirical salvation with healing is that it is a mandate of Christ to be obeyed. This mandate comes from the very will and love of Christ. Thus Jesus empowers and sends his disciples and ourselves both to preach the kingdom and to heal the sick (Luke 9:1-2).

Is this what we are doing as Christian health professionals?

6

Delivery of Total Health Care (Part 1)

Holism Applied to the Church and Ministry

As we have reflected on the dilemmas of the Christian healer, it has become evident that he or she cannot be simply a "treater" of specific ailments but must relate to the whole person. Healing involves bringing about a harmony among body, mind and spirit, and also between oneself and others, between oneself and the rest of God's creation, and between oneself and God.

We can no longer afford to be caught in the compartmentalized dichotomies of Western thought. It cannot be "either/or"—it must be "both/and." This is implicit in the meaning and dynamics of wholeness.

STILL SITTING IN THE DOCTOR'S WAITING ROOM?

Salvation is not just forgiveness of sin—not just redemption and reconciliation. It is not just a moral process that leaves us sitting in the doctor's waiting room—still worried about our symptoms and ailments—after being pardoned. Salvation involves our total restoration. Salvation is transformation to wholeness, just as healing is also a transformation to wholeness. Salvation and healing are the same.

In this chapter we ask ourselves questions that are important to all who minister in Christ's name, but is of particular significance to health practitioners:

· What are the new possibilities for the Christian health-care professional or healer?
· How can a Christian health professional in a practical way go beyond merely being a Christian and coincidentally also a health professional?

NOTHING BUT THE BEST

To respond to this challenge calls for courage. Only our best is good enough.

Let us look at Colossians 3:10-17, 23-24.

And [we] have put on the new nature, which is being renewed in knowledge after the image of its creator. Here there cannot be Greek and Jew, circumcised and uncircumcised, barbarian, Scyth'ian, slave, free man, but Christ is all, and in all.

Put on then, as God's chosen ones, holy and beloved, compassion, kindness, lowliness, meekness, and patience, forbearing one another and, if one has a complaint against another, forgiving each other; as the Lord has forgiven you, so you also must forgive. And above all these put on love, which binds everything together in perfect harmony. And let the peace of Christ rule in your hearts, to which indeed you were called in the one body. And be thankful.

Let the word of Christ dwell in you richly, teach and admonish one another in all wisdom, and sing psalms and hymns and spiritual songs with thankfulness in your hearts to God. And whatever you do, in word or deed, do everything in the name of the Lord Jesus, giving thanks to God the Father through him. . . .

Whatever your task, work heartily, as serving the Lord and not men, knowing that from the Lord you will receive the inheritance as your reward; you are serving the Lord Christ.

Nothing but our best is good enough. Service to God must be in keeping with his desire for totality in salvation and ministry.

But what pragmatic possibilities exist as to how the integration of health care might function at local and regional levels? Let us share some practical suggestions. What we need to have is a total service—involving the total church, delivered by a total team, doing total theology, growing totally and serving the total population with a total clinical approach.

TOTAL SERVICE DELIVERY

Health services should be whole-person in approach, in order to reflect the need for integrated healing.

Mental health care should be in place. On the local church level, a team could be commissioned to provide formal service. The team could include persons such as professional counselors or a psychiatrist. The clergy and well-trained laity would be prepared to provide semi-formal counseling. It has been clearly demonstrated that lay persons can be trained to provide informal or member-to-member counseling.

The church as a healing community and as the advocate for "orphans," as well as for the "enslaved," has a peculiar mission in mental health rehabilitation (see James 1:27 and Luke 4:18). This involves the development of a ministry of the church which will relate to the incapacity and the stigma of severe chronic mental illness and the consequent problems of homelessness and hopelessness.

Sponsoring whole-person services in relation to problems that mental health institutions find difficult to treat is important. These include alcoholism, substance abuse and other addictions, homosexual conflicts, family-member abuse and adjusting to living with HIV/AIDS.

Spiritual health care, which includes the ministry of prayers, confession, spiritual direction, healing rituals and congregational support, should become an integral part of primary health care and hospital facilities. Both psychological and spiritual care should be integrated with the already-existing medical and social-economic services, including community organization. These would be part of a comprehensive scope of promotive, preventive, curative and rehabilitative services. They would stress the vital role of the whole-person issues of wellness, self-responsibility and community building through "others helping others."

This total service is what Christ challenges us to. In Matthew 10:1-2 we are told:

And he called to him his twelve disciples and gave them authority over unclean spirits, to cast them out, and to heal every disease and every infirmity.

Christ gave them a commission to be involved with the spiritual or supernatural by giving them power over unclean spirits. But he also gave them power over the natural—"every disease and every infirmity."

Increasingly, we reflect on the value of traditional healers. We too, need to become traditional healers—traditional Christian healers. This will involve not only using a medical approach in healing diseases, but also using that power which God has given us to heal people spiritually.

THE TOTAL CHURCH

What about the involvement of the total church? The local congregations as healing communities should be influenced by Christian health professionals to function not only as participants and recipients, but also as inter-sectoral collaborators in primary health care. Here, the contribution of the congregation would include total participation, provision of resources in cash or kind, offering volunteer services and participating in need assessment, planning and evaluation.

In some instances, it has been found workable for congregations to be involved individually as sponsors of a complete program, as occurs in Jamaica, where I work.

Another approach would be to have a consortium or pooling of various local congregations within a community, providing together the different aspects of an integrated program, bonded by a jointly sponsored coordinating agency. Alternatively, congregations may choose to play a supporting role to a government or a privately sponsored primary health-care service.

At times, Christian health professionals from various countries have shared with me their concerns about health-care ministry. They feel unsupported, and even alienated, in their local churches. It is vital to keep involved in worship, as well as in general church activities, while sharing and influencing change. One's place is as much in the church as in outside health-care institutions.

The local church holds many advantages in providing a "total service" of whole-person healing. The local church can make it possible for many people in the community to come together. Geographically, it is strategically placed.

The local church is an institution that is involved in ministry at all the life stages of the individual. We have infant baptism or infant blessing. Then we have confirmation, and at adolescence many persons become baptized. Later, we have marriages taking place in the church. When people get older they seek to purchase their own house and may have a house blessing. Then we have the wedding anniversaries. At the end of the course we have funerals.

The church thus is involved in the total life span of the individual. It is where many people find fellowship week after week. And indeed, the church has peculiar rituals and means of health we do not find elsewhere. In the church we find prayers and gifts of the Holy Spirit. We find the exposition of the healing Word of God. Indeed, the church is the bride of Christ, the body of Christ.

In our ministry as health-care professionals we cannot heal without involvement of the total church. As the apostle James tells us,

> Is any one among you suffering? Let him pray. Is any cheerful? Let him sing praise. Is any among you sick? Let him call for the elders of the church, and let them pray over him, anointing him with oil in the name of the Lord; and the prayer of faith will save the sick man, and the Lord will raise him up; and if he has committed sins, he will be forgiven. Therefore confess your sins to one another, and pray for one another, that you may be healed (James 5:13-16).

THE TOTAL TEAM

To be involved as Christian healers we have to use the total team. Given the constant and dynamic nature of the mutual interactions among the physical, spiritual, mental and socio-economic factors, multi-disciplinary teamwork and linkages will become necessary. These would be at the following levels in promotive, preventive, curative and rehabilitative services:

1. Integrated health education and screening.
2. Cross referral and continuous feedback between service staffers involved.
3. Joint monitoring by a case manager.

Services usually are multi-disciplinary and comprehensive. They may easily involve a variety of target populations in whole-person health-care programs. They are probably centered in a local community or congregation, and may well cover both urban and rural regions.

Such services run the risk of having a multiplicity of staff, which they usually cannot afford. There is also the possibility of staff burnout. Both of these factors can threaten the success of a project. Nevertheless, these problems can generally be offset by:

1. Training and employment policies which allow for each staff member to perform more than one role.
2. Policies which facilitate each staff member functioning as a generic whole-person care giver.

In this scenario, every person in the church could be trained as a generic "church health-care worker," with some preparation and expertise in praying, in providing basic health care, in health promotion and in acting as a facilitator of community transformation.

EACH PROFESSIONAL A GENERALIST

Each professional, as distinguished from lay church members, would be equipped as a generalist, as well as functioning in his or her own special area. These professionals would be performing more than one role, including functioning as a generic whole-person care giver.

Michael and Enid Balint and Pietro Castelnuova-Tedesco have provided counseling models for general physicians that are still highly relevant for our purpose here. Lawrence Brammer has done the same for lay workers. Within the Christian tradition, Paul Tournier reflects excellently on the spiritual role of health workers. Francis MacNutt provides useful and simple guidelines for a ministry of divine healing. (Please see "For Further Reading" below.)

Indeed, as we read in 1 Corinthians 12:4-6:

Now there are varieties of gifts, but the same Spirit; and there are varieties of service, but the same Lord; and there are varieties of working, but it is the same God who inspires them all in every one.

Let us not worry about the complexity. Let us, rather, work together as a multi-disciplinary team, because it is one and the same person we are seeking to make whole, and it is the one God who gives to each of us our different talents and skills for the accomplishment of that single purpose.

7

Delivery of Total Health Care (Part 2)

Holism Applied to Theology and Clinic

Unless we understand correctly the nature of realities such as God, humanity, creation, stewardship (both individual and corporate), sin, salvation, healing, life in the Spirit, the church and eschatology, we cannot expect to be effective instruments of healing. All these themes need to be made relevant to the realities which face us in health promotion and care.

To integrate the spiritual with the other dimensions and contexts of healing calls for a constant doing of theology, alongside of any assimilation of anthropological insights and any study of medical and psychological science.

WHAT DOES THE BIBLE SAY?

Health personnel, along with the local congregation, clients and community members, will have to regularly refine their tools of biblical research and working out their understanding of the true nature of the world around them, and particularly, of the persons and personalities they are seeking to help.

How does a Christian missionary, for example, tackle the problem of female genital mutilation, a subject increasingly under discussion? Is it good enough for Western-trained health professionals to arrive in another culture and point out that the practice is bad because of the danger of sepsis?

What we really need to do is to ask why. We need to do some anthropology. Why is it, for example, that these practices have existed? Upon inquiry, we learn that for some tribal people the purpose of this practice is to make it easier for the woman to be faithful to her husband—an objective with which it is not hard to agree.

Fidelity, of course, is a good thing. Having one partner is protection against things such as HIV infection, which are often passed through the man to the woman. We know what the health risks can be, yet we also need to do some theology.

In doing theology, we discover that what we have to say to the involved persons is that the Christian faith addresses the same problem that they are seeking to solve by female circumcision, because the Christian faith also affirms that it is best for us to have one partner. "What therefore God hath joined together, let not man put asunder" (Matthew 19:6). What our theology is saying to the various cultures is that it is God who joins us in marriage, and that it is God who can sustain us and keep us together in "holy" matrimony.

This is only one example. Theological reflection is also needed in areas such as:

• The role of spirituality and liturgy in healing.

- The meaning of issues such as "wholeness," "justice" and ministering.
- The role and function of the church as a healing community.
- Possibilities and methodologies in integrating a biblical theology with everyday life and with modern psychological, medical, sociological and economic concepts.

Work has been done in many of these areas by R. A. Lambourne, a physician-theologian now deceased, the Christian Medical Commission of the World Council of Churches, and myself. Theologians Michael Taylor and Jan Fraser have stressed that for true liberation, theology is best done by the people and at "the base."[1]

BOTTOM-SHELF THEOLOGY

One does not have to become a pastor to do theology. Seminars and courses exist for lay people, and with the guidance of a pastor, one can form a study group of health and community workers such as occurs in the base communities in Latin America and in the Philippines. Each Christian health professional can seek to build his or her own modest theological library.

Learning some anthropology will provide insight to aid conceptual and practical approaches to the religions of non-Christian people. These could specifically relate to how they integrate their spirituality into their own health-care practices. Such inquiry will assist a Christian healer to work with these populations. This would apply to the major religions (such as Islam, Buddhism and Judaism) and to animism, as well as the religious or magical and occult aspects of traditional medicine. One needs to be informed as to "what is" before one can recognize what is compatible with Christianity and genuine healing. One can learn the dangers as well as the advantages.

In the Colossians passage quoted earlier, when we are challenged to do all in the name of the Lord, we are also exhorted to "let the word of Christ dwell in you richly, teach and admonish one another in all wisdom" (Colossians 3:16). In other words, we are challenged to do theology.

GROWING TOTALLY

What about growing totally as Christian healers? This is obviously related to theological "enrichment."

At the psychological and spiritual levels, health personnel and other healers need not only to develop theoretical knowledge but to seek personal growth in terms of self-understanding and interpersonal relations and caring skills. Spiritual growth, in times of personal devotion and in staff retreats, is also a prerequisite for effectiveness in the healing ministry. At the Bethel Center in Jamaica, the staff members have all undergone group counseling and have received training in basic counseling skills.

Let us remember that all of us are wounded healers. Indeed, in Colossians 3:12-14, we are told that we must seek to grow as we "put on compassion, kindness, lowliness, meekness, and patience, forbearing, . . . forgiving each other," and as we "put on love" and "let the peace of Christ rule" in our hearts.

SERVING THE TOTAL POPULATION

To serve beyond the commercialized "medical model" means that we should be healers for the total population, for all who need our help. Again, if "health for all peoples of the world by the year 2000" (the goal of the Alma Ata declaration on primary health care) is to be in any way approximated, priority of service must be accorded to the poor.

The priority of the poor in our spectrum of targeted needs is a much-stated, although oft-neglected, aspect of the church's outreach (see Matthew 25:31-40 and 11:2-5). It needs to become a motivating factor in our ministry of healing.

Furthermore, since wholeness includes an integration of the individual with the human and natural environment, then social, economic and environmental justice becomes a critical health issue.

A TOTAL CLINICAL APPROACH

Our final area of applied holism is in the clinic. We must be involved in a total clinical approach. New types of clinical procedures and skills will become necessary. So will the integration of the spiritual, psychological and socio-economic factors within the physical health-care and healing process.

The kind of total clinical approach which we envision will necessarily include the following two steps:

1. *Taking a spiritual history and making a spiritual diagnosis.* This will allow us to initiate spiritual interventions in our comprehensive services of promotion, prevention, cure and rehabilitation health care.

Spiritual ill-health is alienation from God, who is the being of ultimate importance and supernatural power. The client can be helped to see how this alienation contributes to spiritual guilt and lack of purpose, meaning and moral direction in his or her life. The client can come to see how neglecting the primacy of God in life results in being denied the providence and protection God can provide from evil— whether supernatural, natural or human, from within or from without.

Without God's help, a person lacks the power to transcend self, and thus fails in commitment to others and to the integrity of creation. Alienation from God also leads frequently to existential despair.

General theses such as these will be given specific applications as the client grows in understanding both God and self.

2. *Whole-person history taking, diagnostic formulations and treatment.* At the Bethel Healing Center we do a holistic intake interview. We also focus on precise ways and patterns in which various problems in the respective dimensions interact with each other. Here one would identify patterns such as *vicious cycles* and *linear sequences*.

We look at how much our clients or community members are holistically minded; that is, how much they see themselves in whole-person terms. We help them clarify their willingness to seek integration and their willingness to assure self-responsibility in terms of promoting the wellness of the whole person.

The big question is: How much courage are we willing to muster in order to be involved in this total approach in our services? Only the best is good enough. Are we doing all heartily unto the Lord? Are we providing total service, involving the whole church, delivered by the total team, growing totally, doing total theology, serving the total population and with a total clinical approach?

This is the call of Jesus. Will we be brave enough to commit our faith in total action?

Note

1. R. A. Lambourne, *Community Church and Healing* (London: Darton, Longman & Todd, 1973); Christian Medical Commission, *In Search of Wholeness*, Contact Special series (Geneva: World Council of Churches, 1979); Michael H. Taylor, "People at Work," in *Theology by the People*, ed. Samuel Amirtham and John S. Pobee (Geneva: World Council of Churches, 1986); and Ian M. Fraser, "Theology at the Base," in idem.

8

Delivery of Total Health Care (Part 3)

Holism in Practice—An Example

What does it look like when Christians follow the call of Jesus in this way? In Jamaica, churches from many denominations have established varieties of healing ministries based on the vision of community-based whole-person health. The approach of Bethel Baptist Church shows how one local congregation began a journey of putting faith into action.

THE JAMAICAN CONTEXT

Socio-economic conditions in Jamaica are harsh. For example, in 1991 per capita income was below US$400 and unemployment was 15.4 percent. Adequate health care is beyond the reach of many. When available, it involves unbearably long waits in the lines and on the lists of public clinics and hospitals.

Truly community-based, preventive health care remains inadequate despite significant strides over the past three decades. In fact, early work in proper health care is endangered by a lack of political will.

Unfortunately, community-based consciousness raising, advocacy and empowering are becoming increasingly rare. The legacy of slavery, colonialism and divisions of class and race, along with more recent political patronage and tribalism, has fragmented family and social structures. Religious denominationalism and American-influenced sectarianism also contribute to social disorganization.

More than 70 percent of Jamaican children are born out of wedlock. Women tend to be heads of households, with men being marginal. Internal and external migration have further split families and communities. Violence is a way of life in Jamaican ghettoes, increasingly involving unsupervised teenagers. Eight hundred people died by guns during a year-long political campaign in 1980.

The financial dominance of a small, white-brown commercial elite creates a color-and-class oppression by a minority seen only in South Africa and the Caribbean. Beyond this, external political and economic constraints imposed by first-world bankers and worsened by inadequate local economic management have stifled social justice.

Health professionals and community workers have tended to inherit the authoritarian and condescending attitudes of the colonial system. Black self-hate from slavery undermines togetherness and solidarity. Furthermore, increasing North American values of materialism expressed in a "media colonialism" have undermined commitment to the poor, even in the church.

Indeed, the physical, emotional and spiritual suffering of the Jamaican and Caribbean poor calls for them to be the priority of the church's ministry to the whole person. The gospel involves both preaching *and* healing. This is what Christ sent his disciples to do (Luke 9:1-2).

COMMUNITY-BASED WHOLE-PERSON HEALTH MINISTRY

In 1972, Bethel Baptist Church of Kingston, Jamaica, began a period of theological reflection and planning. The pastor and church council were concerned about having a meaningful outreach program that would minister to the whole person both within the church and in the wider community. The healing ministry began in 1974 as an evening activity, and in 1984 it became established on a full-time basis.

The program is basically a primary health care program with a whole-person approach, that is, having medical, mental health, pastoral and socio-economic service components. It is comprehensive; within each of the above components are curative, rehabilitative and promotive-preventive aspects.

As a community participation-based program, the target populations are clients drawn from the public using the church's holistic health center, an under-served inner city community called Ambrook Lane, and the local congregation. As a congregation-sponsored program, Bethel Baptist Church oversees the ministry, and more than fifty members contribute their time to this ministry.

CURATIVE SERVICES

The Bethel Healing Center (also called the Whole-Person Healing Center) is the main locus of full-time curative services. It consists of medical and mental health facilities along with pastoral and prayer ministries. Each day the healing center begins with devotions in which patients and staff invite God's presence and activity.

Patients see the nurse-interviewer, who listens to complaints and explains the purpose and philosophy of the Center. After using a holistic assessment questionnaire to help the client share problems in all dimensions of life, the nurse performs medical screening. With the patient's consent, the nurse may work with a theological student and a lay person to provide basic mental health and pastoral counseling and pray for healing. A holistic reassessment is carried out on second or third visits of patients.

Next, as needed, clients go to general practitioners and psychological counselors for pastoral counseling and prayer. These professionals may refer patients to the Center's social worker or part-time psychiatrist or, by special arrangement, to outside diagnostic and specialist hospital services. There is also a specialist and a general practice evening clinic run by Baptist volunteer doctors, including those from the church.

Clients then purchase any prescriptions at reduced cost at the Center's pharmacy and pay a consultation fee based on ability to pay. Though contributions are welcomed, the counseling service is free.

At the Center patients receive prayer as well as a prescription. Beyond the prayers of all the staff are those of special prayer counselors from the congregation. A group of parishioners meets weekly to intercede for clients who ask for prayer. The group also prays for the empowering of staff and the resource needs of the ministry.

During 1990 to 1991, the full-time curative medical service had 5,162 patients. The counseling service had 930 clients making 1,324 visits. Use of both services has been growing continuously.

More than 90 percent of attendees are non-members of the church; more than 75 percent are non-Baptists. Though most come from urban areas surrounding Bethel, some clients come from rural areas. The ministry serves a wide constituency.

According to surveys, most medical patients find the service at the Center very satisfactory. Reasons include the approach of the Center's staff and the combination of medical and spiritual care.

CASE STUDY: MARY S.

Mary S. had heard about the Whole-Person Healing Center on her regular visits to church services at Bethel. When her own doctors failed to help her, she decided to seek help at the Center.

I started experiencing chest pains, nervousness and weakness, and I lost a lot of weight, so much so that my husband became alarmed. He sent me to have a thorough check-up. I had blood tests and a chest X-ray, but nothing was found and the symptoms continued. Finally, I decided to try the Bethel clinic. I thought that since the doctors there are Christians, they might be better able to help.

Mrs. S. describes her visit to the clinic:

I first went to the nurse, who asked me some questions. I remember she prayed with me and gave me some advice. Then I went in to see a doctor. It was a female doctor, and she was just as friendly. She encouraged me to talk and listened patiently. I shared with her about a very distressing problem I was having at home. A relative had come to live with us and was making my life miserable.

I made two other visits to the clinic. The doctor helped me to see that my problem was caused by emotional stress; the tension in my home environment was not only a physical one.

I found the clinic a place where people really cared. I felt free to share my problems, which I had not been able to do before. I used to keep everything inside of me because I have no close friends and my husband is very busy so there is no one to talk to. At the clinic, I found friends who listened and prayed. My situation is now changed. I am well again. I have regained the weight I lost, and the pains and nervousness have gone. I am so thankful.

Mrs. S. is now a volunteer worker at the clinic, passing along to others the help she received.

CASE STUDY: ANGELA P.

Angela P. valued the opportunity to receive counseling. She was referred to the Bethel Center counselor when she sought help in controlling her fourteen-year-old son. The thirty-six-year-old mother of three had been separated from her husband for nine years. She explains,

> I was having a very hard time with my son Michael. He had serious behavioral problems. His father and I separated when he was five, and I think this had a bad effect on him. I tried my best with him, but I was not reaching him.

At the time that Ms. P. visited the counselor, she had not been in touch with her husband for years. The counselor suggested she contact him to discuss Michael's problems.

> I didn't take kindly to this suggestion at all, but eventually I decided to try it. As a result, Michael was able to see his father again. This seemed to help him; they developed a relationship which has strengthened to the point that Michael now lives with his father to attend school. He visits me on holidays and some weekends. He is much happier, and his behavior has improved.

Although her immediate problem was resolved, Ms. P. continues to see the counselor. Her regular sessions help her cope better with life.

> I still have many personal problems to work out since my separation and also other areas of my life. Talking one-to-one helps to clarify things for me and guides my decision making. I am particularly happy about the Christian aspect of the counseling given at Bethel. I re-

member that from my very first visit, and ever since that, the counselor prayed with me even before we started talking. I was very impressed with that.

Ms. P. is part of the church now and recommends counseling to others who have problems.

Counseling has helped me cope with the pressure I face as a single mother and also with the difficulties of trying to relate my faith to daily life. If I had counseling earlier, maybe my marriage could have been saved. I know counseling works.

Other clients have reported divine or miraculous healing. One woman's ovarian cyst disappeared, as confirmed by X-ray. A man well known in his village for his disability dramatically regained movement in his right arm. Other practical results of prayer, such as employment and housing, have been reported.

Individuals have also come to find new purpose and meaning in a commitment to Christ, and several have joined various congregations.

REHABILITATIVE SERVICES

The church provides several opportunities for the rehabilitation of clients with socio-economic, chronic physical and mental health problems. Offerings include skill training, craft production, literacy and sign-language classes, and legal and other social services. Church members visit the sick and elderly shut-ins to offer prayer and support.

Bethel has become widely used in the Kingston community for its social rehabilitative opportunities. Hundreds of people have received skill training, remedial education and employment.

Five mentally ill persons have been in our rehabilitation program. Two such persons who had been homeless, were able to join our staff. Most important, several no longer act out the social role of begging and being alien and disruptive. They have been integrated into the church and have become productive members of the fellowship.

PROMOTIVE AND PREVENTIVE SERVICES

The promotive and preventive services have become a major thrust of the Bethel healing ministry. In the healing center, medical and counseling clients participate in wholeness education. The congregation is educated by means of church worship bulletins. For the public at large, there is a letter-answering service in the island's main newspaper.

Twice a year there is a healing Sunday; God's healing activity and prayer are highlighted as a reminder to the congregation. The day includes a health fair for the public. Once a year health-fair activities are extended into a health week. This includes immunization and wellness education as well as screening and education for such ailments as hypertension, diabetes, refractive errors, breast lumps and overweight. Prayer, counseling and referral are provided as appropriate.

Several preventive services are provided weekly for members by the Center:

- For the congregation, there is first-aid training, health education, and family life and personal growth education. These activities include wellness awareness and are promoted through special interest groups such as youth fellowship, women's federation, men's brotherhood and Sunday school.
- Training in counseling is provided for deacons of the church as well as for ninety leaders of the church-sponsored "caring teams." To each of these leaders a given number of church members are assigned for visitation, pastoral care, support, community building and early problem detection and referral.
- Special home health workers have been trained from the membership to visit and care for the sick who are elderly, confined or disabled.
- Couples and individuals from the laity are also trained to offer premarital counseling.
- Single adults and Marriage Enrichment groups carry out self-help educational and support activities.
- Other support activities include house prayer fellowships, intercessory prayer groups and telephone prayer chains.
- A keep-fit class run by the church is available to all.

Thus every member of the church, as well as the public, has access to some promotive and preventive healing activity.

THE AMBROOK LANE COMMUNITY

Ambrook Lane is a low-income community of five hundred to six hundred residents located near the church. It has several problems typical of urban third-world cities. There is a sense of transience, fragmentation, normlessness and lack of formal organization.

The residents have health needs typical of the poor in Jamaica. These include the following:

- Untreated or inadequately treated common ailments of hypertension and diabetes
- Child care problems, including undernourishment, gastroenteritis, inadequate nursery care and early education
- Insect and rodent infestation, uncollected garbage
- Unemployment contributing to undernourishment and inadequate access to health care
- Inadequate youth and sports activities
- Drug abuse
- Juvenile delinquency

In collaboration with residents, several promotive and preventive services have garnered community participation:

- Health activities including education, medical screening, child welfare and growth monitoring, first-aid training, immunization, family planning, and community-health-worker training, as well as informal counseling in nutrition, hygiene and parenting

- Community self-help organization and advocacy in socio-economic and spiritual areas, with the help of a community organizer
- Informal counseling and prayer sessions for problems such as drug abuse and child abuse

There is evidence that the initial apathy and resistance of the people of the Ambrook Lane community is being overcome.

- Aged and ill persons are being visited by community health workers.
- A holistic health-promotion committee has been formed and community health action has been initiated, including health-worker training, child welfare, family planning, community hygiene and nutrition and drama.
- Groups have cleared garbage, fixed pipes and completed a public bathroom.
- Representatives asked city authorities to improve community amenities.
- Residents organized Christmas trees, treats and outings for the children.
- Residents cleared the play area, gained permission to use nearby church grounds and formed a sports club.
- Some residents have begun backyard gardens.
- The community sponsors fund-raising activities.
- Individuals have started small businesses with government help.

- A sewing class for girls has been started and individuals have sought skill training and employment.
- A basic school has been built by residents, over fifty children enrolled and a Parent and Teachers Association formed. Mothers are helping to maintain facilities, and a resident has received training as a teacher.
- A Sunday school and monthly religious services cater to spiritual needs.
- Residents have begun accepting Christ and becoming part of his body.

In addition to the above, parents have demonstrated an increase in knowledge, attitudes and skills in caring for their children. This has been shown in their nutritional status and immunization rate.[1]

Natural community leaders have begun emerging. The self-esteem, self-discipline and self-reliance of community members have improved.

CASE STUDY: MONICA J.

Monica J. has lived in Ambrook Lane for nine years. She is a twenty-two-year-old mother of three small children ranging from one to six years. What is life like in the Lane for Monica?

Not very good. We have many problems, especially housing. Another problem is the lack of water and the surroundings in general are poor.

Monica J. worked as a voluntary health aide in the clinics, run fortnightly by Bethel in Ambrook Lane. Because of her interest and ability, the church sponsored her attendance at a six-month community-health-aide course. She learned how to take blood pressure readings, temperatures and apply dressings. Monica gives voluntary help on clinic days; on other days she often gives help to community members who visit her home.

According to Monica, the clinic has made a big difference to mothers in Ambrook Lane.

Some mothers do not like to go to clinics outside the community and many of them have big children who are not yet immunized. When the church clinic comes, they are willing to go there. Many children have been immunized and the adults get help with their medical problems and medication.

Monica, now a leader and care giver, has gained a new direction in life. She is getting closer to making a commitment to Christ.

ADMINISTRATION

Several elements of the ministry's administrative style help promote its philosophy:

- Mutual consultations, case discussion sessions and overall case management responsibilities are arranged between staff of the various whole-person disciplines. This ensures integration and continuity of care.

- Congregation members volunteer as administrators and workers; more than fifty people serve at a given time. The full range of talents are used. The physician or professional counselor provides professional services. Others may give lay counseling to pre-marrieds, prepare drinks, make posters or provide transportation for sick visitation. Spiritual gifts in ministering and healing are also recognized. The congregation and its leaders are regularly informed of activities and involved in decision-making.

- Patient participation is encouraged. Patients are involved in evaluation surveys and offer suggestions.

- Twice yearly, there are staff retreats for spiritual inspiration, learning and reviewing the ministry's philosophy and activities.

- Staff minister to one another in informal prayer groups and have group sharing sessions led by a chaplain/adviser.

- Despite the need for grants, financial self-help is pursued. Patients are discouraged from expecting totally free service. The church has begun an income-generating program starting with a low-cost lunch service, a thrift shop and friends program.

A MODEL FOR HEALING MINISTRY?

Through consultations and primarily by example, the program at Bethel has influenced the setting up of whole-person health services within most denominations in Jamaica.

S. Copeland[2] reports that in the Kingston and St. Andrew metropolis alone there are at least twenty-nine (mostly part-time) church-related clinics. In addition to volunteers, professional medical workers include sixty-nine nurses, thirty-one physicians, six dentists, eight dental nurses and seven pharmacists. Some 72 percent of clinics use the whole-person model, involving counseling and prayer. Some 57 percent indicated some form of community involvement. Clergy and other staff from these centers have come together to form a national Inter-Church Association of Health, Healing and Counseling Ministries (IA-HHCM).

It is vital to recognize that most healing ministries can function without doctors and professional counselors providing direct services. Nurses, physicians and counselors can train volunteer lay people to do a tremendous amount of ministering through health education, screening and referral, first aid, home care, promoting healthy lifestyles, family life education and marriage enrichment, sharing groups, lay counseling and prayer and visitation activities.

In the Jamaica Baptist Union, for example, more than twenty churches have been able to sustain services largely based on lay counselor and church health worker training programs. The IA-HHCM has been seeking to equip church members in a similar way.

CONCLUSION

The Bethel Baptist healing ministry has been described as an example of church-sponsored, community-based, whole-person health care—an unconventional model of health delivery. Alongside other such efforts in Jamaica, the Bethel work helps offset the distortions of Western thought on the church's and medical profession's view of the person and his or her well-being.

The whole-person approach results in a much wider range of needs being met among client, community and congregation members than would occur in conventional approaches in medical care, community service or church-based ministry. Community-based organizing, consciousness raising, advocacy and self-help approaches may be the start of the spiritual and social liberation of an oppressed community.

The ministry's multifaceted whole-person care and comprehensive primary-health-care emphasis are significantly aided by congregation sponsorship and involvement. Several opportunities are provided for those in the congregation, both professionals and nonprofessionals, to employ their many and various talents and gifts, including those given by the Holy Spirit. Whole-person healing and thus true mission and evangelization are possible because whole-person healing can involve the priesthood of all believers.

Many other Jamaican churches (often independently) have developed healing ministries with varying components of the community-based whole-person health model. This seems to support the viability of this renewed understanding of the church's ministry.

What if all the local churches in the Caribbean were to start at least basic nonprofessional whole-person promotion activities? What if they would recruit and train two lay community health workers and two lay counselors who would integrate whole-person work into their evangelism and local mission outreach? What if every denomination would send whole-person health-related professionals to urban ghettoes, rural villages and to other needy oppressed countries? Then we would be much further on our way to achieving both "health for all by the year 2000" and "the whole church taking the whole gospel to the whole world."

Notes

1. E. Anthony Allen, "Ministering Through Medicine, Counseling and Prayer—A Congregation's Health and Healing Ministry." Unpublished paper, 1989.
2. S. Copeland, "An Analysis of Church Related Clinics in Kingston and St. Andrew and Their Contribution to Healthcare Delivery." Dissertation, University of the West Indies, 1992.

Chapter 8 appeared previously in Transforming Health: Christian Approaches to Healing and Wholeness *(MARC Publications, World Vision International, 1995). The author has additional materials for helping Christians develop whole-person healing ministries. For more information, contact:*

Dr. E. Anthony Allen
Whole Person Resource Centre
8 Durham Avenue
Kingston 6, Jamaica

9

Organizing to Be Healers

Political and Management Implications
of Whole-Person Health Care

It's risky! To attempt to reverse centuries of Western influence in health care is to pick through a cultural, political, sociological, economic and academic mine-field. It can't be accomplished without sacrifice.

In attempting to integrate different disciplines, we run the risk of offending the human structures of each. This puts us in danger of being politically alienated from everybody. Yet, was this not the very dilemma that faced Jesus Christ, who could not be contained in any neat human system of reckoning?

Some of the administrative points of struggle and challenge for political change include the following: professional teamwork, advocacy and dialogue, interdisciplinary training and investigation, and financial courage.

IT WILL TAKE COURAGE

We have already seen that we need to see each person as a whole. And we have seen also that we need the types of services which will promote this wholeness. The question remains, Do we have the courage to do all to the glory of God in promoting such total service?

We must pause at this point to look at how health professionals can organize to be healers. As Christian healers, how do we re-unify health and salvation, and what are the management implications of developing, running and integrating a whole-person health-care program?

Physicians, psychiatrists, social workers and clergy, as well as nonprofessional volunteers and administrators— all these persons have held political power in terms of leadership and economic control in their respective institutions. They will have to be prepared to share their power and resources as they become part of a multi-disciplinary team.

GOD'S STRENGTH PERFECTED
IN HUMAN WEAKNESS

In reality, however, it is as the healer loses his or her power that true healing takes place. We are told in the word of God that "all the members of the body, though many, are one body" (1 Corinthians 12:12) and "the eye cannot say to the hand, 'I have no need of you,' nor again the head to the feet, 'I have no need of you'" (1 Corinthians 12:21).

Likewise, there is no place for the medical professionals to say to those in community development, "We have no need of you," or for the psychologist to say to the social worker, "I have no need of you." It is as the healer loses his or her particular power and allows for wholeness instead of fragmentation that true healing takes place.

Although there were physicians at the time of Christ, he did not heal with the permission of any religious or medical professional establishment or association. Today, such bodies ought to be facilitative and not regulative in function, rather than choosing to be power brokers.

At best, it is difficult for Christian health workers to integrate effectively the spiritual, psychological and socio-economic factors in health-care and hospital services. Without theological inquiry, as well as personal growth, interpersonal caring-skill development and training in community development, it is virtually impossible.

A LONG-STANDING MYTH

For too long, the politics of the establishment—in church, medicine, mental health and social service—have perpetuated the myth that such endeavors are beyond the reach of those who are not clergy or mental-health and social-welfare professionals. Yet these endeavors in promoting multi-disciplinary effectiveness and growth are occurring daily in many settings. Indeed, they are largely responsible for much of the viability of such church-based and other whole-person care services as do exist.

Given the many political obstacles to cooperation at various levels, there is an obvious need for advocacy through dialogue for multi-disciplinary ministry. This needs to be promoted in relation to the various systems of power and influence. Advocacy through dialogue would be directed toward developing joint strategies of inquiry and action in the context of seeking the right of all to receive health promotion and care for the whole person.

John the Baptist had some uncomfortable words to say to persons of different disciplines. When we look at Luke 3:10-14, we see that when the citizens in the commercial sector came to him to ask, "What then shall we do?" he answered, "He who has two coats, let him share with him who has none, and he who has food, let him do likewise." Then the civil servants spoke to him and all sorts of publicans came to him to be baptized, and they too said to him, "Teacher, what shall we do?" His reply was, "Collect no more than is appointed you."

ADVOCACY THROUGH DIALOGUE

Next the professionals in the army came to him, and the soldiers likewise, demanding of him, "And we, what shall we do?" John said to them, "Rob no one by violence or by false accusation, and be content with your wages."

All of John's responses were frank and direct—pointed at curbing the abuse of power in society and at getting people to look out for the interests of others to whom they relate. It was dialogue in the pursuit of altruism. He spoke to their questions, and his answers were challenging. This is our task.

Such advocacy through dialogue would be at the levels of the local community, religion and the nation. And here, doing theology, receiving basic psychological and community-organizational training, and doing theological reflection will prepare the ground for more effective communication between Christian professionals and members of other human-serving disciplines and systems.

Advocacy through dialogue exposes us to the risk of being misunderstood and being ridiculed, but it is the only key to working together successfully.

TRAINING AND INVESTIGATION

Inter-disciplinary training and investigation are vitally important for any health-care worker or related professional who as a Christian wants to become a healer rather than a split personality. It takes a broad inter-disciplinary base to provide appropriate academic and practical training in the fields of physical, mental and spiritual health. Such a base can be provided in a "whole-person core curriculum" in each area of training.

Collaboration may well demand both longer and more rigorous training of service workers, and even some retooling on the part of those teachers responsible for the inter-disciplinary integration. Here again we may encounter opposition to the political sacrifices required for multi-disciplinary cooperation.

Research also is needed in the nature, experiences and effectiveness of historical and existing models of the integrated health-care approach, both generally and in specific cultures. This will facilitate the promotion of successful examples, as well as their refinement and adaptation to local conditions. Are we willing to make this sacrifice in the area of training and inquiry?

FINANCIAL COURAGE

Creative financial planning, rather than pessimism, is necessary to introduce true healing. The whole-person approach to health care, training and research, is going to take extra time. It will take extra personnel. This, together with the fact that spiritual ministry is not usually given on a fee-for-service basis, produces funding difficulties for practitioners in the fields of medicine and psychology, as well as in social work and spiritual ministry. When I share with my medical colleagues how much time it takes at the Baptist Center to receive health and health promotion, the answer usually is, "But how can I possibly manage that in my practice?"

All of this provides challenges in matters of staffing and adequate financing of health-care services. The self-help financial support of the church and local community has been a valuable resource in the case of ours and many other similar projects. Christian relief and development donor agencies with sound co-participatory policies are of immense value.

WHO PAYS THE COST?

Indeed, the Bible states a principle when it speaks about financing services. When Christ sent out the seventy, he said to them that they should not worry about money:

"Carry no purse, no bag, no sandals; and salute no one on the road. Whatever house you enter, first say, 'Peace be to this house!' And if a son of peace is there, your peace shall rest upon him; but if not, it shall return to you. And remain in the same house, eating and drinking what they provide, for the laborer deserves his wages; do not go from house to house. Whenever you enter a town and they receive you, eat what is set before you; heal the sick in it and say to them, 'The kingdom of God has come near to you'"(Luke 10:4-9).

What Christ is saying in these verses is that although it is up to us to take up the charge of proclaiming the kingdom, and healing the sick, that this has financial implications. The laborer is worthy of his hire, and thus the community members also have a responsibility for the proclamation of the kingdom and the healing of the sick.

I ask, however, if our agencies and Christian health professionals are willing to make such a financial sacrifice?

Contributors at all levels will need to recognize that whole-person services may cost more in the short term. Yet nothing comes without cost. And indeed, in the long term, the resulting greater degree of wholeness achieved by persons, families and communities will result in lower recurrent costs. Are our agencies and Christian health professionals willing to make the financial sacrifice?

To ignore all the political, training and management implications we have discussed here will lead to problems. It will frustrate the smooth transition to a type of healing care that has until now been too alien. Too many health professionals and health-related institutions in both the northern and southern hemispheres have been too long under the influence of compartmentalized Western thought. Change will not come easily. Are we prepared to count the cost?

10

Empowerment of the Christian Healer

Loving and Receiving and Other Keys
to Effective Ministry

The challenge to whole-person healing is before us. The organizational problems are formidable. But what about personal equipment for the task?

At the risk of sounding mystical, I venture to state that the way of being a healer of the whole person in community is the way of contemplative spirituality in the midst of activism. As we seek to be active in obeying God's mandate to preach the kingdom and heal the sick, we need to be engaged in loving God and receiving spiritually from God.

OBSTACLES IN A HEALING MINISTRY

Obstacles to ministry will always abound. As healers, we have to be aware of this. This reality is brought into focus in the story of the disciples who at the mountaintop shared with Christ in the glory of his transfiguration, but down in the valley were stopped cold with their own limitations.

And when they came to the crowd, a man came up to him and kneeling before him said, "Lord, have mercy on my son, for he is an epileptic and he suffers terribly; for often he falls into the fire, and often into the water. And I brought him to your disciples, and they could not heal him."

And Jesus answered, "O faithless and perverse generation, how long am I to be with you? How long am I to bear with you? Bring him here to me."

And Jesus rebuked him, and the demon came out of him, and the boy was cured instantly. Then the disciples came to Jesus privately and said, "Why could we not cast it out?"

He said to them, "Because of your little faith. For truly, I say to you, if you have faith as a grain of mustard seed, you will say to this mountain, 'Move from here to there,' and it will move; and nothing will be impossible to you" (Matthew 17:14-21)

Indeed, there are several obstacles to the seemingly impossible challenges involved in community-based, whole-person healing—obstacles of severe physical suffering, the psychological bondage of addictions, personality problems, the emotional pain of anxiety depression and psychosis. Oppression in the socio-economic sphere leads to poverty, discrimination, racism, social disorganization, war, crime, violence and abuse in families.

The obstacles of spiritual evil occur in the form of secularization, loss of spiritual values, occult practices and propaganda for the purpose of destroying others, mind controlling and the activity of evil spirits to tempt, oppress and control. Existential despair and loss of meaning and purpose of life are other forms of spiritual evil.

One can also experience lack of management resources for ministry—manpower, money, materials, motivation, training, political will—and indeed the obstacle constituted by the fact that we are all wounded healers.

LOVING AND RECEIVING
IN CONTEMPLATIVE SPIRITUALITY

Loving and receiving from God (which we have chosen to call contemplative spirituality) are the only way to overcome the obstacles faced in a healing ministry. Loving and receiving from God take us beyond the first steps of conversion.

In Acts 2, St. Peter shares with us that to turn our backs on (or repent from) an undesirable lifestyle and rejection of God, and to become initiated into the communion of believers by the symbolic act of baptism are only the first steps in the Christian life. On the day of Pentecost many people asked him, "What shall we do?" He answered, "Repent and be baptized." But he went on to say, "and you shall receive the gift of the Holy Spirit" (Acts 2:37-38). The fullness of spiritual experience comes only with being filled with God's presence in the person of the Holy Spirit.

There are two aspects of relating to God's Holy Spirit as we seek to be a ministry team. The first is obvious: *receiving the Spirit*. That is, asking the Spirit to come and live within us. Receiving the Spirit occurs as we make our commitment to Christ, as we ask Christ to be our Lord and Savior.

Yet this is not necessarily enough; we could say, "Lord come into my life," and still not be significantly transformed or empowered for ministry.

AN EVIL INTRUDER

The fable is told of a man, who, when Christ came knocking at his door, said to him, "Come into my house, Lord, and I will give you a room where you can stay. Just stay in that room." Then some days later, the Evil One came to his door and knocked loudly. And when he opened the door, the Evil One came in and created havoc in his house.

Then the householder said to Christ, "Lord, how is it that you are in my house and yet all this has happened?" And Christ said to him, you did not give me the keys to every room in your house."

The man then said, "Lord, I will give you all the keys. Here is the key to my living room. Take charge of my entertainment. I give you the key to my bedroom—take charge of my sexuality. I give you the key to my dining room—take charge of my eating habits. I give you the key to every room in my house—you take charge of my whole house."

And then, a few days later, again came a loud knocking at the door, and one could hear the babble and chatter of all the demons of Satan. He had come with all his reinforcements. But it was Jesus who stood and opened the door. Immediately, the devil and his demons retreated in disarray, shouting, "Lord of hosts, Lord of hosts!"

Shall we then appreciate the difference between just asking the Spirit to come in and *asking the Spirit to fill us com-*

pletely, in order that we be completely governed by him? To walk in the Spirit is to be completely governed by the Spirit. It says in that wonderful chapter eight of Romans, where the teaching about the Spirit of God is expounded, "For they that are of the flesh are governed by the things of the flesh, but they that follow the Spirit are governed by the Spirit."

Thus, being completely governed by the Spirit (Romans 8:5) in one's mind—thoughts and actions—or being filled and walking in the Spirit, means that the Spirit is not merely received and present but is given total access to every room and corner of the "house" of our lives in order to do his work of transforming, empowering (Galatians 5:4, 16-25; 1 Corinthians 12:4-11), teaching (John 14:26) and leading (Romans 8:14, Acts 13:2).

GOALS OF LOVING AND RECEIVING

We are told that as we long for the Spirit—as we seek to receive him—*we shall receive his power and spiritual gifts.* According to Luke 9, when Christ sent out his disciples, the first thing that he did was not to give them a plan or strategy, but rather he gave them "power and authority over all demons and to cure diseases" (v. 1). And then he sent them out.

Again, when Christ was leaving them after his resurrection, as he gave them the "Great Commission" he said to his disciples, "But you shall receive power when the Holy Spirit has come upon you; and you shall be my witnesses . . . to the end of the earth" (Acts 1:8). As part of his power,

God gives to his Church supernatural gifts for ministry (1 Corinthians 12:4-11, 28).

Receiving God's power and also loving God involves receiving God's love and grace. God's love is unconditional and forgiving (Ephesians 2:4,5). God's love is for all: "For God so loved the world that he gave his only Son, that whoever believes in him should not perish but have eternal life" (John 3:16). God's love is totally sacrificial (Romans 5:8). God loved us and gave himself for us. We love God because God first loved us and gave his son to die for us.

God's love is what leads to his grace, his undeserved favor that meets all our needs, whether spiritual, psychological, social or economic. It is of that grace that the writer to the Philippians can say, "And my God will supply every need of yours according to his riches in glory in Christ Jesus" (Philippians 4:19). God's love and grace are made effective by the power of his Spirit (1 Corinthians 12:9). To him is given all power in heaven and in earth (1 Chronicles 29:12).

DISCIPLINES OF LOVING AND RECEIVING

Like anything else, the loving and receiving aspect of spirituality involves specific steps, and these steps can be seen as disciplines, inasmuch as they require persistent and constant application—daily, if possible.

We are free to develop our own steps in the life of contemplative spirituality. The steps I will share are identified by the initials or acronym LBSL, "Leaving Behind Self and Loving." The steps are as follows:

L - *Loving* God with our whole person
B - *Believing* in God and in his power, love and grace through the Holy Spirit
S - *Surrendering* to him
L - *Listening* to him

Loving God with our whole person means, "and you shall love the LORD your God with all your heart, and with all your soul and with all your might" (Deuteronomy 6:5). This is a daily act of adoration, of thanksgiving and indeed, of self-giving in absolute loyalty. It is saying to God, "All I am is yours."

This is similar to the total devotion of one human being to another. It is a loss of self-centeredness to become God-centered. It is the giving of our possessions as well as of ourselves (Luke 14:33). The rich young ruler was told that if he wished to have eternal life, he should "sell all that you have and distribute to the poor . . . and come, follow me" (Luke 18:22). We are talking here about total giving.

Believing in God is next. As we love, as we adore God, we come to believe in his power, love and grace, operating through Christ and the Holy Spirit. This is the main part of effective living—not depending only on our own efforts (Ephesians 2:8-10). It leads to the miraculous power of the Spirit in us (Galatians 3:15).

We are told that whoever comes to God must believe that God is a real person, one who rewards those who diligently seek him (Hebrews 11:1-6). We need to believe "for we are not contending against flesh and blood, but against the principalities, against the powers, against the world rulers of this present darkness, against the spiritual hosts of wickedness in the heavenly places" (Ephesians 6:12). Wholeness and becoming healers are in the realm of spiritual warfare.

Believing can indeed lead to the miraculous power of the Spirit working within us. As Christ said,

> "Truly, truly, I say to you, he who believes in me will also do the works that I do; and greater works than these will he do, because I go to the Father. Whatever you ask in my name, I will do it, that the Father may be glorified in the Son; if you ask anything in my name, I will do it. If you love me, you will keep my commandments. And I will pray the Father, and he will give you another Counselor, to be with you for ever" (John 14:12-16).

Matthew 21:22 tells us that whatever we ask in prayer, if we have faith, we will receive. When the disciples were powerless to cast out a demon, Christ said to them that if they would only believe, "all things are possible" (Mark 9:23).

Then there is *surrendering to God*—surrendering our efforts and frustrations with the recognition that while we are limited, God is limitless (Mark 10:27). Surrendering is a confession of our having failed God, others and ourself. Surrendering is a turning away (repenting) from the ways in which we have failed God, others and self. Surrendering is "letting go and letting God."

> Have no anxiety about anything, but in everything by prayer and supplication with thanksgiving, let your requests be made known to God. And the peace of God,

which passes all understanding, will keep your hearts and minds in Christ Jesus (Philippians 4:6-7).

Let go and let God. It is like exhaling and inhaling. Think of that when you think of surrendering. In letting go, the burdens will become light (Matthew 11:28). It is to let go so that we cease to live, so that Christ can live in us (Galatians 2:20). And as we let go, and as we "inhale" and "let God," it is a surrendering and opening of self in order to be filled by God's presence through his Holy Spirit. Christ says:

> "And I tell you, ask and it will be given you; seek, and you will find; knock, and it will be opened to you... If you then, who are evil, know how to give good gifts to your children, how much more will the heavenly Father give the Holy Spirit to those who ask him!" (Luke 11:9-13).

We ought to *listen to God*, having loved him and celebrated his presence; having believed that his love, his power and his grace can operate in our lives; having "let go" to "let God." In our contemplation we now listen, while asking, "Lord, what do you have to say to me?" This is the most vital aspect.

Most of my life I have thought of prayer as just talking, talking, talking. It is only recently that I have come to learn that prayer also involves listening and more listening. "Lord, what do you have to say to me?" It is only then, as the Spirit fills us, as we surrender, as we listen, that the Spirit will guide us when to minister, even in the middle of a disaster, how to minister, how to manage our projects, how to deal with ourself.

The Spirit of God speaks to us through the words of Scripture (2 Timothy 3:15-17), speaks to us directly through our meditating in silence—not the earthquake, not the wind and not the fire, but through that "still, small voice" (1 Kings 19:11,12). As the Lord used Ananias and sent him to Paul, who had just had his conversion experience (Acts 9:17), so God speaks to us through the words of others.

He spoke to Peter through a vision to go to the Gentiles (Acts 10:19). God may speak to us also through dreams and visions. Hebrews 2:4 mentions that God spoke through Jesus, with words confirmed by the words of the disciples and demonstrated by "signs and wonders." And the miraculous unfolding of circumstances, the miraculous action of God in our lives, is yet another way in which he speaks to us. God also speaks to us through angels. Let us not limit the ways in which we can experience listening to God. Let us be open to the many channels God can use to reveal his will and purposes to us.

PRACTICAL AIDS

What are some aids to help us love God, believe in him, surrender to him and listen to his voice?

Prayer

Prayer is the most important activity in the discipline of contemplative spirituality. Christ said to his disciples that faith and the power they needed to overcome evil come only by prayer and fasting. Prayer should involve adoration, thanksgiving, confession, intercession and supplication—waiting on God and listening, if we are to hear him.

Bible study

Alongside prayer, comes *Bible study*, involving a daily listening to God through his Word. Also, there is silent *meditation*—finding a quiet place, as Christ himself went "apart" to be alone.

Journaling

Another form of support is *writing a journal*, putting down on paper our burdens, what God says to us, and what we say to God in our prayers. We can come back from week to week and month to month and review the journal and be inspired and reminded of God's power and grace.

Sharing

Community is the greatest human agent of healing and spiritual growth. Therefore we need a *prayer partner* and/or a *small group* of brethren with whom we can share. In a small group, the gifts of the Spirit, such as prophecy and healing, can be used. In inspirational *retreats* our teams can come apart for a while to listen to God.

Fasting

Fasting is a valuable discipline to accompany all the others, because "this kind [of demon] goeth not out but by prayer and fasting" (Matthew 17:21, KJV).

OBEDIENCE

Obeying God as we listen to him is the pathway to effective ministry because it offers us the challenge of following through on what we hear from him when we listen.

Obedience is an expression of love which leads to a greater presence of God within us. Where there is obedience, we find our new selves, a new direction, a new transformation, a new effectiveness in ministry.

Out of loving, believing, surrendering and listening, there comes transformation, commitment, renewed motivation and empowerment. Indeed, although with men the task may seem impossible, with God all things will now be possible. But "this kind" of power comes only by prayer and fasting.

It is only in this way that health and salvation—which are the same—shall be revealed to the world. How willing are we to love God, to believe in him, to surrender and listen to him? How willing are we to seek the path of contemplative spirituality as we face obstacles in our ministry?

11

Summary and Conclusion

Wholeness as the "Cinderella" of Health Care

We have said that "semantics is praxis," and in asserting this, we have pointed to the confusion that has abounded in the Western-influenced health-care systems and within the Christian church—confusion about the meaning of the words "health" and "salvation." As we have seen in our own experience, more than a few Christian health professionals have experienced a problem of identity. We have tended to be living contradictions or "split personalities."

The great divide in caring for aspects of a whole person has created a crisis in modern health care.

I have suggested that a rediscovered understanding of health as "wholeness" constitutes an approach that is truer to science, to human reality and thus to the Bible. This perspective calls for us to be Christian healers rather than health professionals who merely happen to be Christians. We have tried to share the true biblical meaning of salvation as relating to God's action for the whole person and all aspects of life. To see transformation to "wholeness" or "abundant life" in Christ as the ultimate work of the cross is to span the great semantic divide and once again recognize healing as salvation.

This recognition calls for us to pursue healing not as a "secular" exercise, but as a total ministry of evangelism by demonstrating and proclaiming. It will point to the kingdom of God as a divine reign with empirical, or measurable, manifestations.

RIGOR IN REASONING IS CALLED FOR

Rediscovering health as wholenesss and healing as salvation demands rigor in reasoning and in biblical exegesis as well as innovation in practice.

We have sought to establish that the problems in integrating mental and spiritual health begin at the level of faults in Western culture and philosophy, which we need to overcome. These inherited dichotomies prevent the bringing together of the presumably separate conceptual points of departure and the seemingly different methodologies of the physical, psychological, spiritual and social aspects of human life.

We have attempted to outline briefly these points of departure. We have also illustrated the dynamic relationships in health and illness: between the person as a biological object, the person as a subject interacting with himself or herself, with others and with the environment, and the person as spirit relating to God, the ultimate meaning and the ground of all being.

Practical possibilities for the Christian healer and for the Christian health professional have been outlined, relating to whole-person services which involve local congregations as healing communities. These would be largely promotive and preventive, run by well-linked multi-disciplinary teams, where most persons would function as generic whole-person care givers. Participating personnel will need to do theology and to seek personal growth in self-understanding and in inter-personal caring skills. Services would cater to mental health problems. Spiritual management approaches would also be necessary.

Policy, training and management issues that relate to risky "political" or power implications have been outlined, as have the relevance of culture, economic issues and academic aspects. Advocacy through dialogue across disciplines, and within institutions of influence, has been recommended. This will facilitate inter-sectoral cooperation and the protection of rights.

The question is: How much flexibility exists in medicine and psychology, on the one hand, and in the church, on the other, in order to effect the necessary changes? The church itself has been somewhat guilty of a Cartesian dualism and tends to be polarized between the material and the spiritual.

THE CHURCH WAS NOT BORN IN THE WEST

The fact is, despite its recent historical tendencies, the church did not originate in Western culture. It came out of the background of God's dealing with the Hebrew people, who gained their cultural understanding from his relationship with them.

Despite its inner tensions, many sections of the church have continued to be faithful to God's mandate to heal the sick as a part of proclaiming the gospel. Indeed, following the example of Christ, from time to time in history a number of churches, denominations and Christian health professionals have seen the healing of the sick as the natural accompaniment and fulfillment of the proclamation of the kingdom of God.

The Christian health professional of today needs to be a healer. To this end, he or she will have to be a bit of a lay philosopher and theologian. He or she will also need to be an innovator, enabler and facilitator for the church, a trainer, a community builder and an advocate. It goes without saying that this should be the generic pattern for the lay healer, as well.

We are involved with broken persons and systems, as well as with human and spiritual resistance. As we face our own brokenness, we will need to engage in the contemplative spirituality of loving God and receiving from him. This spirituality needs to be concurrent with our activism. We will receive power for the "impossible" as we engage in loving God, believing his Word, surrendering and listening in our personal and corporate meditation, study, prayer reflection and waiting upon him. This will lead to a renewed and more effective obedience.

It is time for Cinderella to be discovered as the real "queen of the ball." Wholeness must not remain the poor stepchild of health care and evangelism. Wholeness must claim its rightful place if we are to:

- see health care truly resulting in "health for all by the year 2000";

- seek, with God's help, the way of spiritual renewal for all, leading to justice, peace, and the integrity of creation; and
- see the earth "filled with the knowledge of the glory of the Lord, as the waters cover the sea" (Habakkuk 2:14).

AN UNPARDONABLE OVERSIGHT

No longer can wholeness be the unrecognized "Cinderella" of health care and evangelism. This failure of recognition cannot continue if health care is truly to lead to "Health for all by the year 2000," and if with God's help we are to seek the way of spiritual renewal for all, as well as justice, peace and the integrity of creation.

In other words, it is time for Cinderella to be identified as the real queen of the ball. Wholeness cannot remain the undiscovered princess of health care and evangelism if we want to see the "earth . . . filled with the glory of the LORD as the waters cover the sea" (Habakkuk 2:14).

A Contemplative Meditation on the Lord's Prayer

Let us meditate. And as we seek in this act of meditation to love God, to believe in him, to surrender to him and to listen to him, let us reflect on the words of the Lord's Prayer, which Jesus taught his disciples.

LOVING

Lord, we love you because you are *Our Father*, Papa, Daddy. You first loved us. You are our Father whom we adore because you are lifted up, you are transcendent, *you are in heaven*, holding the whole world in your hands. As we love you, we acknowledge your might. We say that your name is special. *Your name is holy*, as we love and adore you.

BELIEVING

Lord, we believe in you, because *your kingdom has come* on earth. We are now in your kingdom. You are our king.

As king, you have total authority in the land. Thus whenever we seek anything and we proclaim anything in your name, it will be done. Yours is the name above all names— the name to which every knee shall bow above the earth, on and under the earth. Your kingdom is come.

SURRENDERING

And Lord, we surrender to you as we say, *let your will be done on earth*, in our homes, in our neighborhood, as we sit by ourselves, in our thought-life, in our work, in our play, in every aspect of our life, as in our morality. In every aspect we surrender, that your will may be done here *as it is in heaven.*

Lord, as we "let go" we want to "let God," so we say to you, give us what we need to live. Supply what is necessary to meet the personal and practical needs of ourselves, of the people whom we serve, and of the whole world. Lord, *give us this day our daily bread.*

And as we seek your presence in our lives when we "let go" to "let God," we also have to seek your forgiveness for the many ways in which we have failed you. We lay bare before you the sins of pride, lust, doubt, hatred for others, greed and jealousy. We confess the more private sins of lack of temperance and the sins that for each one of us only we as humans may know about. As we confess to you now, each one of us, we say *forgive us our trespasses.*

And as we "let go," help us, Lord, to let go the wrong that others have done us. We find it hard to forget the pain of the heart, but Lord, we ask you to heal the heart, to help us let go and forgive, to enjoy that freedom in our spirits. So as we let go, Lord, *help us to forgive.*

And as we let go, we pray that you will protect us from the testing that will overwhelm us. Lord, we will experience sickness, yes. We will experience loss, yes. We will experience persecution, yes. We will experience inner doubt and affliction from the evil one, yes. But Lord, like Job, we can say, "After my skin has been thus destroyed, then from my flesh I shall see God" (Job 19:26). Lord, we know that you will not give us more than we can bear. And even though we walk in the valley of the shadow of death, we shall fear no evil, *you will not lead us into overwhelming temptation* and testing because you are our Lord and you will comfort and *deliver us from evil.*

LISTENING

Lord, as we "let go" in these moments, now help us to listen to you, to hear what you have to say to us.

Let us now open our minds and hearts to hear the Lord.

(*Silence.*)

Let us love the Lord absolutely. He loves us absolutely. We celebrate the words he has said to us. And we celebrate these words because we say, "Lord as we have loved you, as we have believed you, as we have surrendered to you, as we have listened to you, we now seek to obey, because *yours is the kingdom, the power and the glory, forever and ever. Amen.*"

For Further Reading

Allen, David F., ed. "Whole-Person Care: The Ethical Responsibility of the Physician." *Whole-Person Medicine* 21-42. Downers Grove: InterVarsity Press, 1980.

Allen, E. Anthony, Kenneth L. Luscombe, Bryant L. Myers and Eric R. Ram. *Health, Healing and Transformation: Biblical Reflections on the Church in Ministries of Healing and Wholeness.* Monrovia: MARC Publications, World Vision International, 1991. Includes biblical expositions by the author on healers and healing.

Allen, E. Anthony. "A Whole-Person Health Ministry: The Bethel Baptist Experience, Kingston, Jamaica." *Contact* No. 113. Christian Medical Commission, World Council of Churches, Geneva, 1990.

Anderson, Robert G. "A Model for Liaison with Clergy." *Hospital & Community Psychiatry.* 29, 800-2, 1978.

Anderson, Robert G. "The Role of the Church in the Community Care of the Chronically Mentally Disabled: Reclaiming an Historic Ministry." *Pastoral Psychology* 28:38-52, 1979.

Bakken, Kenneth L. *The Call to Wholeness.* New York: Crossroad Publishing, 1985.

Balint, Enid and J.S. Norell, eds. *Six Minutes for the Patient: Interactions in General Practice Consultation.* 1st ed. London: Tavistock, 1973.

Balint, Michael and Enid. *Psychotherapeutic Techniques in Medicine*. 1st ed. London: Tavistock, 1961.

Brammer, Lawrence M. *The Helping Relationship*. 3d ed. Englewood Cliffs: Prentice-Hall, 1985.

Castelnuovo-Tedesco, Pietro. *The Twenty-Minute Hour*. 1st ed. London: J. and A. Churchill, 1965.

Christian Medical Commission, World Council of Churches. "In Search of Wholeness." *Contact*. Special Series 2, Geneva, 1979.

Christian Medical Commission, World Council of Churches. *Healing and Wholeness: The Churches' Role in Health*. Geneva: World Council of Churches, 1990.

Dubos, René. *Man Adapting*. 1st Edition. New Haven: Yale University Press, 1965.

Eastwood, M.R. "Epidemiological Studies in Psychosomatic Medicine." In Z. J. Lipowski, et al. *Psycho-Somatic Medicine* 411-20. New York: Oxford University Press, 1977.

Engel, G.L. "The Need for a New Medical Model: A Challenge to Biomedicine." *Science* 196:99-136, 1977.

Fraser, Ian M. "Theology at the Base." In Amirtham, Samuel and Pobee, John S., ed. *Theology by the People*. Geneva: World Council of Churches, 1986.

Giel, R. and Hardin, T.W. "Psychiatric Priorities in Developing Countries." *British Journal of Psychiatry* 128:513-22, 1976.

Griffith, Ezra E. H., et al. "Possession, Prayer and Testimony." *Psychiatry* 43:120-28, 1980.

Griffith, Ezra E.H., et al. "An Analysis of the Therapeutic Elements in a Black Church Service." *Hospital and Community Psychiatry* 35:464-96, 1984.

Harding, T. W. "Mental Health and Primary Health care—The Role of the Village Healthworker." Unpublished manuscript, Brazzaville, 1979.

Hoebel, E. Adamson. *Anthropology: The Study of Man.* 3d ed. New York: McGraw-Hill Book Co., 1966.

Kelsey, Morton T. *Healing and Christianity.* 1st Edition. London: SCM Press, 1973.

Lambourne, R.A. *Community Church and Healing.* London: Darton, Longman & Todd, 1973.

Larson, D. B. and S. S. Larson. *The Forgotten Factor in Physical and Mental Health: What Does the Research Show?* Arlington: National Institute for Healthcare Research, 1992.

Lewis, John. *History of Philosophy.* 1st ed. London: The English Universities Press, 1969.

MacNutt, Francis. *Healing.* 3d ed. Notre Dame, Indiana: Ave Maria Press, 1974.

Milsum, John H. "Lifestyle Changes of the Whole Person: Stimulation Through Health Hazard Appraisal." In Davidson, Park O. and Sheena M. Davidson, eds. *Behavioral Medicine: Changing Health Lifestyles,* 116-50. New York: Brunner/Mazel, 1978.

Nottingham, Elizabeth K. *Religion and Society.* 12th ed. New York: Random House, 1964.

Peaston, Monroe. *Personal Living.* 1st ed. New York, London: Harper & Row, 1972.

Rahe, Richard H. "Epidemiological Studies of Life Change and Illness." In Z. J. Lipowski, et al. *Psycho-Somatic Medicine* 421-34. New York: Oxford University Press, 1977.

Ram, Eric R., ed., *Transforming Health: Christian Approaches to Healing and Wholeness*. Monrovia: MARC Publications, World Vision International, 1995. Includes two chapters by the author.

Starr, Paul. *The Social Transformation of American Medicine: The Rise of a Sovereign Profession and the Making of a Vast Industry*. New York: Basic Books, 1982.

Taylor, Michael H. People at Work." In Amirtham, Samuel and Pobee. John S., ed. *Theology by the People*. Geneva: World Council of Churches, 1986.

Tournier, Paul. *A Doctor's Casebook in the Light of the Bible*. London: SM Press, 1973.

Tubesing, Donald A. *Wholistic Health*. New York: Human Sciences Press, 1979.

Wilson, Mitchell. "DSM-111 and the Transformation of American Psychiatry: A History." *American Journal of Psychiatry* 150:3, 399-410, 1993.

World Health Organization. *The WHO Medium-Term Mental Health Program 1975-1982*. Geneva: WHO, 1978.

World Health Organization. *Alma-Ata 1978 Primary Health Care Declaration*. Geneva: WHO, 1978.

MARC

Bringing you key resources on the world mission of the church

MARC books and other publications support the work of MARC (Mission Advanced Research and Communications Center), which is to inspire fresh vision and empower Christian mission among those who extend the whole gospel to the whole world.

Recent MARC titles include:

▶ *By Word, Work and Wonder: Cases in Holistic Mission* by Thomas H. McAlpine. Thoroughly explores the question of holism in Christian mission and brings you several case studies from around the world. $15.95

▶ *Serving with the Poor in Asia: Cases in Holistic Ministry*, T. Yamamori, B. Myers and D. Conner, editors. Well-known mission leaders comment on cases in holistic mission presented from seven different Asian contexts. These cases and analyses help us better understand what a holistic witness to the gospel of Christ means today. $15.95

▶ *Transforming Health: Christian Approaches to Healing and Wholeness*, Eric Ram, editor. Explores the many methods God uses to brings about health and wholeness in today's broken world. $21.95

▶ *God So Loves the City: Seeking a Theology for Urban Mission*, Charles Van Engen and Jude Tiersma, editors. Experienced urban practitioners from around the world explore the most urgent issues facing those who minister in today's cities. $21.95

▶ *Healing the Children of War*, Phyllis Kilbourn, editor. A handbook for Christians who desire to be of service to children who have suffered deep traumas as a result of war. $21.95

▶ *Survival of the Fittest: Keeping Yourself Healthy in Travel and Service Overseas* by Christine Aroney-Sine. A useful traveling companion for anyone venturing overseas, complete with a pre-trip medical checklist.
$9.95

Order Toll Free in USA: 1-800-777-7752

▶ *Women as Leaders: Accepting the Challenge of Scripture* by Katherine Haubert. Examines Scripture related to the question of leadership roles for women in the church to allow you to reach your own conclusions about this important and timely topic. $8.95

▶ *The Changing Shape of World Mission* by Bryant L. Myers. Presents in color graphs, charts and maps the challenge before global missions, including the unfinished task of world evangelization. Also available in color slides and overheads—excellent for presentations!

Book..$5.95
Slides...$99.95
Overheads.......................................$99.95
Presentation Set *(one book, slides and overheads)* $175.00

▶ *Patching God's Garment* by W. Dayton Roberts. Skillfully shows how the environmental crisis affects the church's evangelistic mission and calls Christians to assume leadership in the field of environmental protection.
$13.95

▶ *Focus! The Power of People Group Thinking* by John D. Robb is a practical manual for planning effective strategies to reach the unreached. This expanded and revised edition includes important new material on prayer and networking as keys to mission progress. $10.95

Ask about the MARC subscription—get all of MARC's 1996 titles at a discount. Makes a great gift for your favorite missionary or pastor!

Ask for the MARC Newsletter and complete publications list

MARC A division of World Vision International
121 E. Huntington Dr. • Monrovia • CA • 91016-3400

Visa and MasterCard accepted

Order Toll Free in USA: 1-800-777-7752